Christmas
around the world

Christmas
around the world

Lesley Sims

Illustrated by Angelo Ruta

Additional illustrations by
Anna Luraschi and Brenda Haw

Reading Consultant: Alison Kelly
Roehampton University

Contents

Chapter 1   Christmas time   5

Chapter 2   Deck the halls   13

Chapter 3   Piles of presents   24

Chapter 4   Food and fun   36

Christmas cookies to make   46

Chapter 1

Christmas time

It's the night before Christmas. Everyone is fast asleep, waiting for the magic to begin.

Cards are written and sent.
Presents are wrapped and
waiting under the tree.

Stockings hang empty
from the mantelpiece, while
children dream of a secret
visitor and a sack, bursting
with surprises...

People have been
enjoying Christmas for
over 2,000 years.

Early Christians started it, to celebrate the birth of Jesus Christ. Jesus was born in Bethlehem, a small town in the Middle East.

His parents, Mary and Joseph, were visiting the town, but every inn was full. So Jesus was born in a stable. A star shone brightly overhead to show everyone where he was.

Excited shepherds working in nearby fields came to see him. Then three wise kings arrived from far-off lands to worship him – and they all brought presents.

Now, Christians go to church on Christmas Day to remember Jesus's birth, but millions of others celebrate too.

Chapter 2

Deck the halls

Early in December, the
streets sparkle with
lights. Christmas
is coming...

The four weeks leading up to Christmas are known as Advent. An Advent calendar counts down the days, from December 1st to Christmas Day on December 25th.

The Sunday before Advent used to be called Stir-up Sunday, because it was the day people made Christmas puddings. Everyone stirred the pudding and made a wish.

Today, most people buy
their Christmas puddings, but
they still decorate their homes
with flickering candles and
holly, just as people did
hundreds of years ago.

Then they add strands of
glittering silver tinsel and put
up twinkling Christmas lights.

Some people hang up mistletoe too – first used by the Celts over 2,000 years ago. The Celts thought it was a magical plant of love, so today we kiss under it.

And front doors display wreaths woven with leaves and shiny balls.

In Germany, Christmas markets are set up for people to buy decorations. A Christmas market is called a *Weihnachtsmarkt.**

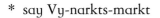

* say Vy-narkts-markt

Some of the stalls sell
Christmas cookies for people
to eat while they shop, and
hot spicy drinks to keep
them warm.

The brightest decoration in every home is a sparkling tree, topped with a fairy, a star or a Christmas angel.

The first
Christmas trees
hung in Eastern
Europe – upside down.
An old legend says the
idea to decorate them came
from Martin Luther, a
German priest.

One night, he saw
stars twinkling through
the trees. Back at
home, he lit up
his tree with
candles.

Now all over the world
people decorate their trees.
The American president
switches on the lights
of a tree outside the
White House...

...and a giant tree shines out in Trafalgar Square, in London – a gift to Britain from Norway.

Chapter 3

Piles of presents

Gifts have been part of Christmas ever since the kings and shepherds brought presents for Jesus.

Families and friends buy each other presents, but other people bring them too...

Long ago in Turkey, there lived a bishop named Nicholas.

Nicholas loved to give children presents and help the poor. He was such a good man he became St. Nicholas. Today he's known as Santa Claus – or Father Christmas.

A story about St. Nicholas: why stockings are left out

There was once a man who had three daughters, but he was too poor to pay for their weddings.

"We'll never be married," sighed one, as she washed their stockings and hung them over the fire to dry.

St. Nicholas was walking by and heard her. Late that night, he dropped a shower of golden coins down the chimney.

When the sisters found the gold in their stockings, they were thrilled.

Their father was delighted. "It must be a gift from St. Nicholas," he smiled.

Some say that Santa Claus lives at the North Pole, or in Lapland, which is nearby.

Every year, millions of children send him letters, saying what they'd like in their stockings for Christmas.

Santa packs his bulging
sack and sets off on his sleigh,
pulled by nine flying reindeer.

Santa isn't the only person to bring presents at Christmas. Italian children wait for *La Befana*, a kind, old witch.

She didn't join the kings to visit Jesus, because she had to sweep her house. Now she searches for the baby every Christmas, leaving presents as she goes.

In Sweden,
children leave out a
bowl of porridge for the
Tomte, a gnome who lives
under the floorboards.

Children in Syria
leave out hay, for the three
kings' youngest camel. In the
morning, the hay has vanished
and presents are there instead.

In Germany, children write letters to a Christmas angel called the *Christkind*, asking him to leave their presents under the tree.

People open their presents at different times too. In Holland, the paper is torn off on St. Nicholas's Day, December 6th.

In Scandinavia and Germany, Christmas Eve is the big night. Then Christmas morning is free for church and visiting friends.

But in Britain, Australia, the United States and many other countries, everyone has to wait for Christmas Day.

For hundreds of years, presents came without cards... until, in 1843, an artist named John Callcott Horsley invented the first ever Christmas card.

Now, more than ten thousand million Christmas cards are sent every year.

Chapter 4

Food and fun

Every Christmas, families and friends get together to enjoy an enormous dinner. What they eat depends on where they live.

Menu

Roast turkey
Belgium, Brazil, Britain, Ireland, Nigeria
and the United States

Boiled cod in a creamy sauce
Finland

Spicy chicken stew
Ethiopia, in Africa

Roast eel
Italy

Roast pig
Philippines

Dessert

Christmas pudding

People in Britain eat this rich, spicy pudding. It's filled with fruit and lucky charms. Long ago, people put all kinds of charms – from sixpences and silver rings to buttons and tiny dolls – in their puddings for luck.

Rice pudding

In Denmark, people eat a
pudding of rice and milk, with a
lucky almond cooked in it.

Panettone

In Italy, people enjoy slices
of a tall, sweet, yellow cake.

For most people, Christmas is a holiday. With the presents unwrapped and all the food eaten, they can do whatever they like best...

...which may be going for a winter walk, playing games or snoozing in front of the TV.

In Alaska, children run through the streets, carrying a star on a pole. Everyone else tries to steal the star.

Mexican children try to smash a *piñata* – a clay container. As it breaks, tiny presents tumble out.

And, all over the world,
people go carol singing.
They gather in the street or
walk from house to house,
singing Christmas songs and
collecting money for charity.

Carols are full of hope,
telling listeners to be kind,
just like Jesus.

The first carols began as jolly Christmas dances in Italy, nearly 1,000 years ago. The dancers started singing along and carols were born.

Christmas lasts for twelve days. There's even a song about it, with presents for each day.

On the first day of Christmas,
my true love sent to me
a partridge in a pear tree...

44

January 6th is *Epiphany*. This celebrates the day the kings came to see Jesus, so some countries call it Three Kings' Day.

People eat Kings' cake and give each other gifts. And then Christmas is truly over.

Christmas cookies to make

This is a recipe for *Lebkuchen,** Christmas cookies from Germany.

Ingredients

1 egg
100g (¹/₂ cup) brown sugar
100g (¹/₂ cup) honey
100g (¹/₂ cup) golden (corn) syrup
400g (3 cups) plain or all-purpose flour
¹/₂ teaspoon each of ground cinnamon, ground nutmeg, ground cloves and ground allspice
¹/₂ teaspoon baking soda or bicarbonate of soda
Tubes of ready-made (writing) icing

What to do

1. In a large bowl, mix the egg, brown sugar, honey and syrup together.
2. Sift the flour, spices and baking soda into the bowl.
3. Stir until the mixture is a soft dough.

* say **layb**-coo-khen

4. Roll out the dough on a floured surface until it's 1cm (½ inch) thick.
5. Cut out hearts and Christmas shapes using a cookie cutter.
6. Arrange them on a greased baking sheet, at least 2cm (1 inch) apart.

Bake in an oven at 350°F (180°C or gas mark 5) for 12 minutes.

When the *Lebkuchen* are cool, decorate them with icing and eat them.

Research by Anna Claybourne

Edited by Jane Chisholm

Cover design: Russell Punter

Christmas card on p34 © Handout/Reuters/Corbis

First published in 2005 by Usborne Publishing Ltd., Usborne House,
83-85 Saffron Hill, London EC1N 8RT, England. www.usborne.com
Copyright © 2005 Usborne Publishing Ltd.